THE
AWAKENING

A Devotional For The Youth In Perilous Times

Palesa S. Mhlongo

The Awakening: A devotional for the youth in perilous times

Published by Palesa Sarah Mhlongo

Fochville, South Africa

endtimepublications1@gmail.com

ISBN 978-0-620-89641-2

2 4 6 8 10 9 7 5 3 1

Layout and cover design by Boutique Books

Printed in South Africa by Digital Action

TABLE OF CONTENTS

FOREWORD

"**The Awakening: A Devotional For Youth in Perilous Times**" is a much needed resource for the youth who live in the world that is riddled with challenges that include among others: Gender Based Violence (GBV), Drug and alcohol abuse, violence at home and in the community, a plethora of political and social issues, lives centered on selfishness and self-centeredness, trying to live in a globalized world where shifting economies and automation has rendered many of the youth incapable of finding employment. The adversary of our souls since the entrance of sin, has been pursuing the youth in order to make sure that they are destabilized from focusing on those things that matter and that are of eternal consequence, mainly by bringing suffering so as to suggest that God does not care enough for the plight of the youth as they navigate through this difficult world.

The author of this book has attempted through topics such as: "Remember judgment", "Prayer: The breath of the soul", "Learn to be quiet", "Make a U-turn", "Gratitude to God: A healthy you" and "The great awakening call" to conscientize the youth to remember that they are not invincible unless they return to God as per His invitation that is all encompassing. The youth of today may never know what lies ahead of them but they cannot be oblivious to the fact that the God of their parents holds both yesterday, today and tomorrow into eternity with Him. In this book, the youth are therefore encouraged not to panic or be intimidated by evil forces but to remain faithful to God for He is their source of comfort and strength. They are called to return to the Lord, in these perilous times.

May the God of heaven, the Almighty, bless the youth as they follow the steps of those who have travelled this road before and to be humble enough to learn from their strength and weaknesses while forging ahead with their Christian faith. As the youth navigate through these uncertain days, may they move ever forward in faith, trusting God who does not err nor can He ever abandon those whose trust is in Him. Remembering that their safety is not in their self-reliance but in God who is their Hope, Protector and their Shield.

May those who open the pages of this book and read them with understanding, be blessed with wisdom and the ability to implement whatever is contained herein.

DR. DINGINDAWO PAULUS SHONGWE
D.Litt et Phil, Rand Afrikaans University
(Now University of Johannesburg)
President of the Seventh-Day Adventist
Church in the Trans-Orange Conference

PRELUDE

We live in a time characterized by busy schedules; many people move about to and fro, trying to make a living. A time when many do not sleep, striving to think about new business ventures. A time when a vast majority sacrifices so much just to make it to the top. Young people are greatly committed to so much, yet divided effort is devoted to celestial endeavours. It is a sad reality that many of us have put the pleasures of this world as a priority. Many are dying; many are born. Many have plenty and many are in utter poverty. Many accept the Lord as their Saviour and many deny Him unashamedly. Where is godliness, righteousness, and a relationship with God? These are all put as last and least imperatives. We cannot be comfortable with a tremendously shallow relationship with our Maker. We simply cannot settle for less when it comes to righteous living. The Word of God speaks directly about perilous times and the signs of the Second Coming of King Jesus. We are surely living in the end of times and we cannot afford to live as we please. This devotional is meant to engage the youth in matters of spiritual vigilance. The title of this devotional, *The Awakening: A devotional for the youth in perilous times,* is inspired by Romans 13:11, which reads: *"And that, knowing the time, that now it is high time to awake out of sleep: for now is our salvation nearer than when we believed."* This is a call to be vigilant, sober-minded and to awake from spiritual sleep. If you are a young person and you are reading this prelude, know that this book is meant to move you from your comfort zone. You are not to be the same again after reflecting on the content of this book. This work is meant to awaken you to the reality that, God's standard of character is lofty, and He will in no way lower it for our comfort. However, there is hope, the standard is unquestionably attainable. In her book, *Messages to Young People (page 15)*, Ellen White has this to say: *"As we walk day by day in the light He sends us, in willing obedience to all His requirements, our experience grows and broadens until we reach the full stature of men and women in Christ Jesus."* God is interested in the spiritual growth of the youth, He has bestowed great gifts into their hands so that they may be co-labourers with Him in His vineyard. It is my prayer that we may draw closer to God now more than ever before, may we realise that there is time no more. Jesus once asked a vital question: *"… Nevertheless when the Son of man cometh, shall He find faith on the earth?"* (Luke 18:8b). May Jesus' coming not find us wanting! For the next forty days and beyond, make the Bible your companion and righteousness your God-directed and aided quest.

~ *Palesa Sarah Mhlongo*

DAY 1

Amnesia in youth

Who created you? Do you ever pause for a moment to ponder upon the complexity of your body's design? Are you aware that the One who created your incomprehensible brain is the same One who gives you life? My dear friend, GOD created you. The same God who formed and fashioned this universe. The same One who spoke heaven and earth into existence is OUR Creator. The wisest man of all times, King Solomon, gives us a very earnest counsel: *'Remember now thy creator.'* This is the same man who asked for wisdom from the Lord and he knew very well as you and I do, that in our youth we are committed to a great deal of things. It is sad though that most of these things are hardly about the Lord and His mission. You would agree with me that in this day and age, young people are living haphazardly, they are living carefree lives. The inspired Word of God indicates that, as a result, there is propensity to forget the Lord during youthful days. Nowadays, it is as if there is no God. Fear for God has faded in this generation, the youth do according to their heart's desires; substance abuse and crime amongst others are the rule of the day. Neglect of Bible study and commitment to spreading the gospel are saved for last. Fashion trends are followed to the letter. If only we could take a moment to think intensely about Jesus Christ's sacrifice on the cross, then we would grasp the fact that He suffered and died for our sake. We would realise that it is to Him alone that we should offer our full devotion. It is true that one will not be young forever, old age will come (by the Lord's mercies). Who wants to spend their old age in regret? Sadly, the hands of time cannot be turned back. If we forget the Lord, soon we will be under the control of the devil; that is bondage at its best. In such a state we will not find pleasure in life, we will desire to die because we would no longer endure such suffering though it was self-inflicted. Dear youth, spare your life by seeking to serve the Lord, seek to know Him as your personal Lord and Saviour. In your daily endeavours draw closer to Him, choose to let Him lead your life and you will not be lost. By the grace of God, a committed young person will manage to flee youthful amnesia.

Personal Reflective Probe

1. Is my life showing evidence of youthful amnesia where I seem to have forgotten my Creator?
2. What things contribute to this amnesia?
3. How can I best draw more closer to the Lord in my youth?
4. How will I help another to avoid the same pitfalls?
5. What new perspective have I gained from today's lesson?

DAY 2

Remember judgment

> *"Rejoice, O young man, in thy youth; and let thy heart cheer thee in the days of thy youth, and walk in the ways of thine heart, and in the sight of thine eyes: but know thou, that for all these things God will bring thee into judgment" ~ Ecclesiastes 11:9*

This is one of the most half-read scriptural texts in the Bible and because of this, most young people ruin their lives and claim that 'God wants them to enjoy their youth.' It is plain truth that God wants us to be joyful. It pleases Him when we are at peace, but it is against His will for us to endanger our lives, all in the name of fulfilling Scripture. The word of wisdom tells us that the Day of Judgment is coming and each one of us will be accountable for his or her own works. Allow me to tell you dear friend, that God wants us to delight ourselves in Him and in Him alone; it is contrary to His commandments for us to waste our lives in *inter alia* alcohol and promiscuous behaviour. Psalm 37:4 says, *'Delight thyself also in the Lord; and He shall give thee the desires of thine heart.'* When you find your joy in the Lord and not in the things of this world, you will receive what you desire. Your life will be pleasing to God because you are led by Him. A young person who is led by the Lord will not make decisions that will put his or her life in jeopardy. I am certain that if you give your life to Jesus Christ, He will be the ruler of your heart and the ways of your heart will be piloted by Him. There is no way that your life can be characterized by disorder if Jesus is your leader. Think about it. Also keep in mind my friend, that you will be accountable to the Lord concerning what you have done with your precious youthful days. Will this be an account worthy of a crown or destruction? This lies in your hands and it starts now. Have a desire to be among those who will be waiting for the appearing of Jesus so that they may ascend with Him to the heavenly mansions. You ought to start shaping your character now so that it is well-fitted for heaven but O dear youth, this is not formed through pursuing the patterns of this perverse world. It is only attained if we become like Jesus in our words, thoughts, and deeds; if only we are clothed with His righteousness which is freely available from Him. Franklin E. Belden rightfully asks in this moving hymn: *'How shall we stand in that great day? Shall we be found before Him wanting? Or with our sins all washed away?'*

Personal Reflective Probe

1. What is my most-prized takeaway from today's lesson?
2. How will I warn other young people of the coming judgment?
3. How do I intend to structure my life henceforth in preparation of the Second Coming of Jesus?
4. Do I believe that I can attain much through the help of Jesus Christ?

DAY 3

Heart response

"Only fear the Lord, and serve Him in truth with all your heart: for consider how great things He hath done for you" ~ 1 Samuel 12:24

Our Father, Creator of heaven and earth and all the inhabitants thereof is truly worthy to be praised! He does great and wonderful things in our lives, yet we do not see Him with our naked eyes. We can all testify that this world does not function autonomously but there is One who is in control, sustaining us and everything around us – This is God and none other. Until you have a personal experience with Him, you will not understand it when I say He is ALL IN ALL. God is amazing, He has done so much for me personally, and I am confident that you also have an experience of how He has led you in the past and how He continues to do so even today. He hears us when we call upon Him and He provides our daily needs. You need to be mindful of the fact that it takes faith for God to be real to you as an individual. Yes, He does not always come to us in ways we expect, but He surely gives us the very best all the time. You need to believe that He is who He says He is because it does not please Him when we doubt His power. When our faith in God wavers, we will not obtain the blessings that can only be attained through unwavering faith. Now that God has been so good to you, what is it that you are doing for Him? He is speaking to us today, as

He spoke through the prophet Samuel to the Israelites and He says: *'Only fear the Lord, and serve Him in truth with all your heart.'* Our God is a jealous God, He requires all humanity to fear Him (honour Him) because He is the only true God. To fear Him means that you acknowledge His omnipotence (all-powerful), His omnipresence (all-present), and His omniscience (all-knowledgeable). This means that we must come to the realisation that we can never hide ourselves from Him, our words, thoughts, and deeds whether good or evil are ever before Him. When we fear Him, loving Him with all our hearts we will be inspired to serve Him with our all. Many a times we devote our energies and capabilities on things that have nothing to do with the kingdom of God. How sad! Will you now fear and serve the Lord with all your heart? Will you forsake the things of this world and tell others what He has done for you?

Personal Reflective Probe

1. What has the Lord done for me?
2. Is my life of service to God?
3. Who will I tell of the Lord's blessings in my life?
4. Do I really fear God?
5. What new perspective have I gained from today's lesson?

DAY 4

The gulf

Oftentimes we pray to God asking for various needs and wants. We tend to feel like He does not take note of our requests. We usually feel like there is a huge distance between us and God because in time past people like Moses could talk to God and hear Him reply, but that is not the case today. Is He still the same God? (See Malachi 3:6 for an answer). You may be asking, dear young person: 'Why is God not responding to my prayers?' The Holy Spirit, through the prophet Isaiah makes us aware that our sins have put a gulf between us and our Creator. It is imperative for us to remember that God hates sin because it was sin that made Him give away His only begotten Son to die for the world. The Lord is not pleased when we harbour sins in our hearts and approach His throne with unrepentant hearts; He wants us to confess and turn away from our evil ways. He requires us to be perfect as He is perfect, but you need to know that you can never attain perfection on your own, through your own strength. You need the Lord; you need to surrender to His will and allow Him to transform you. '*... and your sins have hid His face from you, that He will not hear*' (Isaiah 59:2b). My friend, through the help of the Holy Spirit let us take a moment each day, pause from our busyness and consecrate ourselves to the Lord and ask Him to cleanse us from all unrighteousness. If we do not do this, neglecting our duty toward Him, we will not hear Him speak to us. We need to be so close to the Lord, that even our requests are in line with His will, without us having to worry about anything. He says that we should abide in Him and He will abide in us (see John 15:4). We can do nothing without Him, we will never overcome sin without His enabling power and a gulf will ever exist between us and Him. The call is plain and assuring: *'Come unto me...'* (Matthew 11:28).

"The yielding of self, surrendering all to the will of God, requires a struggle; but the soul must submit to God before it can be renewed in holiness" (Steps to Christ by E.G. White, page 43*).*

Personal Reflective Probe

1. What things have come between God and I?
2. Do I believe that Jesus' death on the cross makes it possible for me to reconnect with God?
3. What will I do differently henceforth, by the grace and aid of God?
4. What new perspective have I gained from this lesson?

DAY 5

Prayer: The breath of the soul

Imagine yourself trapped in a very dark room, all doors are locked, all windows are closed and cannot be opened in any way. There is not even a tiny hole from where fresh air can penetrate; you have no food and water. You will be stuck there for a while unless somebody comes to your rescue. How long do you think you will survive in such an environment? Life Sciences teaches us that our bodies need water and oxygen for us to survive but not only these two, food is also essential. We are also taught that our bodies constantly release carbon dioxide. Now answers to the above question may differ, but the main point is, when we breathe, oxygen needs to come into our bodies and we are to release carbon dioxide. Again, imagine that you are due to fight Satan, a spiritual being and you cannot see him with your naked eyes. Which weapon will you use to fight him? The Word of God tells us that our battle is not against flesh and blood but against principalities and powers of darkness[1]. Allow me to submit to you that our spiritual life is in jeopardy without prayer because we need strength from the all-powerful God so that we may fight evil. Prayer is indeed the breath of the soul and without it, we may be spiritually 'dead-walking' thus the devil will do all that pleases

---

1   See Ephesians 6:12

him with our lives. It is for this reason that we should pray without ceasing[2] (without end), we need to be well-armed for the spiritual warfare. Prayer also draws us close to God, enabling us to have peace that surpasses all understanding[3]. *'Prayer is the opening of the heart to God as to a friend. Not that it is necessary in order to make known to God what we are, but in order to enable us to receive Him. Prayer does not bring God down to us, but brings us up to Him'* (Steps to Christ, p.93). If you have been spending time whining about everything, start investing that time in sincere prayer to the Lord and experience joy unspeakable, peace beyond human comprehension and love unconditional. The Lord who neither slumbers nor sleeps is ever waiting to hear from us and when we pray in faith, we will receive the petitions we ask of Him. Faithful is He who has promised. Finally, the Lord does hear the petitions of converted young people too.

Personal Reflective Probe

1. What does prayer mean to me?
2. In my own assessment, am I spending enough time in communion with God?
3. How will I now improve my prayer life?
4. When I pray, what things do I mostly pray about?
5. How can I learn to start praying for others more than I do for myself?

---

2   See 1 Thessalonians 5:17
3   See Philippians 4:7

DAY 6

Pristine in Christ Jesus

The word 'pristine' simply means 'new'. This is one of the most sobering assurances you can find in the Bible and I am certain that you are already asking yourself: How possible is this? Can Jesus Christ really make me a new person regardless of the sins I have committed? Let me hasten to say that God does not lie nor does He make promises that He cannot fulfil. The same Jesus who is speaking to us through Paul is the same One who created us therefore we can trust His word. It is an undeniable fact that our past lives may not be appetizing if they were to be brought to light in the present. I also know for a fact that Satan is in the business of making us dwell much on the wrong things we have done or that we continue to do, so that we may lose sight of what God can do for us and through us. The Word of God says that when we are in Christ, we are new creatures. We start off a new journey with Him and we forsake the things of old. Mind you, this portion of scripture will only be a cliché if we simply recite it and not believe it. We need to turn away from our wicked ways and commit ourselves to Jesus Christ and to Him alone. Do not allow the evil one to tell you that you are already used up and good for nothing; you should confidently proclaim the fact that you are pristine in Jesus Christ and the old 'you' has been done away with. Have faith in God and with all your heart, believe that He is who He says He is and you will see the great things He will do in your life. You will be able to overcome sin every single day rather than spending time feeling guilty about all that you have done in the past. Allow Christ Jesus to make you new, let Him restore His image in you.

> *"If you see your sinfulness, do not wait to make yourself better. How many there are who think they are not good enough to come to Christ. Do you expect to become better through your own efforts?" (Steps to Christ, p.31)*

Personal Reflective Probe

1. Do I truly believe that Jesus can make me a new creature?
2. What things am I still holding on from my past?
3. What is my takeaway from today's lesson?

DAY 7

Jesus, Our Righteousness

> *"For as by one man's disobedience many were made sinners, so by the obedience of one shall many be made righteous"* ~ Romans 5:19

We are all born into sin because our first parents (Adam and Eve) sinned before God and we suffered the consequences thereof. Due to our sinful nature, we commit sin even when we are not aware of it; that just shows our sinful state. The Bible tells us that by *'one man's disobedience many were made sinners...,'* the text does not say that many 'chose' to be sinners. All those who were born after the man 'Adam' took of the same nature without having to choose. You do not have to do anything to be declared a sinner but you just have to be born and it is so. To Adam was entrusted stewardship of this world and all that is in it, but he chose to disobey God. It is for this reason, that we are facing so much suffering in this world. I praise the Lord that the statement does not end there because then it would mean that humanity would not have a chance to enter into the kingdom of God. *'By the obedience of one shall many be made righteous'*; this is our greatest hope: the righteousness that is only found in Christ Jesus. We know that only Jesus could live as a human being, be tempted in all points and yet He never sinned (He obeyed God completely). It is only the righteousness of Jesus that we need for us to inherit His kingdom because in and of ourselves

~ 23 ~

we are totally incapable. What we need to do is to cling on to Jesus and humbly ask for His cleansing so that we may be pure. Our first parents failed to obey God, but Jesus Christ showed us that it is possible to live a holy life thus He invites us to come to Him so that we may receive of the same blessing. When we are in Christ, sin no longer has any power over us, we are justified by faith. When Satan accuses us of sinning, Jesus stands before us as our Mediator and we are not condemned. Believe that you can only obtain salvation from Jesus and commit yourself to daily follow Him – believe that He is your Righteousness.

> *"But let none deceive themselves with the thought that God, in His great love and mercy, will yet save even the rejecters of His grace" (Steps to Christ, p.31).*

Personal Reflective Probe

1. What does righteousness mean to me as an individual?
2. How can I be clothed in Christ's righteousness?
3. What principles have I drawn from today's message?
4. How can I best share this message with those who believe in self-righteousness?

DAY 8

Down to earth

We live in an era whereby people are so in love with being in high positions; people want to be recognised. Many a people do not mind the kind of businesses they engage themselves in, if only they get status and money then all is well. As Scripture has prophesied centuries ago, many are *'lovers of their own selves'* (see 2 Timothy 3:2) and this is happening right before us. One would even murder for the sake of a position in this world. Pride has increased exponentially and guess what, some even want to take God's position in order for them to be prominent, loved and honoured by the world. Humility seems to be a very obsolete trait, those who humble themselves are considered the lowest in society. When you humble yourself, you are despised, and people take that for foolishness. I encourage you to rejoice, because in actual fact, God is pleased with you, contrary to popular practise. God requires those who are called by His name, His children, Christians, to humble themselves before Him because He is the Supreme God. Dear friend, you need to know your place and give God the place that is due to Him because if you lift[4] yourself up, your dismal downfall shall soon follow. Let

---

4   See James 4:10

God place you in high positions where He knows that you will serve Him rather than doing it yourself for selfish desires. Remember that Lucifer (who is now Satan) fell from heaven[5] because He wanted to be above God, he was not willing to humble himself and let God occupy His well-deserved seat. This tells us that all those who are hungry for positions of this world, who would stop at nothing to get what they want, are only but instruments of Satan. I am certain that you have chosen to be on God's side, therefore seek to be far away from pride and humbly follow where the Lord leads you. I know that the narrow way may not seem inviting, it may not make you famous but it sure will give you a much greater position in God's kingdom – your reward is not of this world, it is eternal. Pride only leads to destruction, for it 'comes before falling'.

Personal Reflective Probe

1. Am I a humble person?
2. How can I best shun being proud?
3. How will I make others aware of the importance of humility?
4. What can I learn from Jesus' humble character?
5. What is my takeaway from today's message?

---

5   See Isaiah 14:12-14

DAY 9

Whose face?

"... and pray, and seek my face..." ~ 2 Chronicles 7:14

Today, the world is full of people who love themselves so much that they always want to be on the spotlight; they want to be known for their beauty, their intellect and socio-economic status. It is also common that when there is a well-renowned person in town, many will flock just to see the celebrity and even shake his or her hand. The face, however, says a lot about a person. You learn whether the individual is sad or angry by assessing their face. There is something about people's faces that interest others, the so-called beautiful faces make it to the cover page of a magazine and the headlines of the most-viewed television programmes. This often leads to idolizing other human beings. In essence, we are so much interested in getting to know more about other people instead of God. The Lord is pleased with those who desire to know Him personally because then He would show forth His power so that He will be glorified. Have you ever asked yourself: How does God look like? Well, that is really a mind-boggling question. You will have to be part of the number of the saints who will go to heaven to experience that superb sight – seeing the face of God! The Creator of heaven and earth is Supreme, He is big and none of us would live were we to see Him face-to-face. It is the Lord's *face* we are to seek, and the only source of this kind of endeavour is the Word of God. Through the word, we learn of God's character and through the Holy Spirit we are inspired to have a desire to be like Him – God's face is His character; who He is. When we know who He is, we will know what He expects of us and because we already have a close relationship with Him, that would not feel like a burden to us but joy. It is about time that we cease pursuing the fame of this world but rather seek after who God is and ask Him to transform us. We may look up to certain people due to their godly characters, but have we realised just how their existence is also dependent on God the Creator? Anytime they may cease to live and our hopes will be tarnished. However, if our goal is to know the Lord and serve Him with our all, then we will not be disappointed because *'God is not man that He should lie'* (Numbers 23:19) and He never ceases to exist. Ask yourself today: Whose face am I going after?

Personal Reflective Probe

1. Whose face have I been seeking?
2. What is my understanding of 'the face of God'?
3. How will I practically start to seek God's face?
4. Am I willing to make God priority in my life henceforth?
5. How will I help others grow their relationship with God?

DAY 10

Make a U-turn

God is so merciful, He always presents us with opportunities that will enable us to have life eternal. He cares so much about us that it does not please Him when we are lost, living lives that are detrimental to our destiny. The Lord hates sin so much that at one point He is going to destroy it eternally. However, He does not want us to cling onto sin lest we partake of its destruction. When you turn, you face a different direction and that is what the Lord wants us to do: to turn from our wicked ways. I usually define this using the actual U-turn scenario in real life; when you are driving on the road, at some point you may need to make a U-turn because of an urgent reason. You could be lost or in need of going back to where you came from for whatever reason, but you will not use the exact same lane you used. You will travel the opposite direction, on a different lane because there will be oncoming traffic on the same lane you used. The point is, the Lord requires us to leave the route that is leading us to destruction and get onto the one that will give us life eternal. He wants us to forsake our evil ways, totally turn away from them and pursue holiness and Godlikeness. Once again, we cannot do this on our own – we need to surrender ourselves to the Holy Spirit and let Him work in us that which we cannot do in and of ourselves. It is the Spirit of God that opens our eyes and allows us to see our sinfulness and puts in us a longing to walk in the path of righteousness. We may choose for ourselves, God never compels anyone to follow Him. It is important for us to notice that if we do not turn away from our wicked ways we shall bear the unpalatable results thereof: death instead of eternal life with the Father.

"Repentance includes sorrow for sin and a turning away from it. We shall not renounce sin unless we see its sinfulness; until we turn away from it in heart, there will be no real change in the life" (Steps to Christ, p. 23).

Personal Reflective Probe

1. What things do I need to repent from in my daily living?
2. Do I believe that I can be transformed through the help of Jesus?
3. How will I share this message with others?
4. How can I ensure that once I have repented, I do not swallow back my vomit?
5. What important lessons have I gained from today's message?

DAY 11

Learn to be quiet

Our tongues really get us into some serious trouble, don't they? Human beings never get tired of talking; we also want our side of the story to be heard; we want our ideas to be adopted. In situations that stimulate feelings of anger, we often talk without thinking carefully. Ultimately, one is hurt because of our unrefined comments. Hearts are broken. Relationships are put to an end. Regrets are breakfast, lunch, and supper. A *Tswana Proverb* reads: *"Lefoko ga le boe, go boa monwana"* (Loose translation: "A finger may be retracted, but not words"). What you say to a person may be in their minds for a very long time. The Word of God speaks of meekness as a fruit of the Spirit, we need to learn to be meek in all circumstances. Meekness[6] simply means being of a quiet spirit, avoiding verbal and non-verbal clashes with people. It is the kind of virtue that leads one to be quiet even in situations where one ought to be retaliating. This is a virtue that only Jesus Christ possessed when He was here on earth, and I believe that He can grant it to us if we ask Him in faith. Our tongues ought to be very far from gossip because that does nothing except to undermine other people.

---

6   See a more detailed definition on https://dictionary.cambridge.org

We gain nothing from talking too much, not considering how the next person will feel like upon hearing that negative statements were uttered about him or her. The Lord says that if we desire to be out of trouble, we should 'keep our mouths' meaning that we should guard what comes out from there, we should think prayerfully about what we want to say to the other person. Let God put into your mouth words that are seasoned with love, care and tenderness so that they may give life to another. Furthermore, you should also take note of the fact that we can either build or destroy with our tongues (See James 3:8, 10), therefore strive to please the Lord with your words. If you have nothing uplifting to say, rather be quiet, according to Scripture you will be saving yourself a lot of trouble. If we are to be examples to those who do not know the Lord, we need to have His character – it is all possible for those who yield their will to Him and let Him guide their way. God is able when we fail.

Personal Reflective Probe

1. What is my weakness when it comes to using words?
2. What consequences followed the use of unkind words in my life?
3. How will I begin using kind words towards others?
4. What can I learn from Jesus' meek character?
5. What important lessons have I gained from this message?

DAY 12

Sufficient grace

We truly serve an amazing God, He loves us unconditionally and for this He must be praised because He is totally deserving of that. God is not like us humans who at times perceive ourselves to be better than others; He is a gentle Father who loves us all the same way. We know that there are people who usually withhold their grace from those who have hurt them. This is a vengeful spirit and it is not of God. When you have wronged someone, God, through His Holy Spirit, will convict you of your wrong and you will be led to ask for forgiveness. When you take the initiative to ask for pardon, grace may be withheld from you because the other person will feel that you have hurt them and thus you deserve to feel pain as well. The question is: does this please God? He is a gracious God and He requires those who are called by His name to be gracious as well. The Lord says that His grace is sufficient. He is ever waiting for us to approach His throne with humility, acknowledging that we are weak. Furthermore, He mentions that when we are weak, His strength is made perfect. Have you ever felt like you are totally weak? When you are weak, all that you need is strength and God offers perfect strength if only we have faith in Him. When our loved ones are reluctant to grant us grace when we have wronged them, God says that His grace is sufficient. While the Lord is still near, while He can be found, we ought to plead for His grace in our lives so that we may be fitted to enter into His kingdom. Keep in mind that time is coming when the door of mercy and grace shall be shut and Christ Jesus will come on earth to take His own. Use the moment you have now to draw closer to the Lord and serve Him with all your heart *while it is still day*. The Lord is ever present to save us when we are sinking. He requires that we fully believe that He is an all-powerful God who has all that we need. Do you not sometimes wonder why is it that God has tolerated you so much for the awful things you have done in the past? You look at yourself today, honoured by many, loved by many and considered one of the most generous people ever. Ultimately you say: It was all because of God's amazing grace!

Personal Reflective Probe

1. What is my understanding of God's grace?
2. Do I have a personal experience of the grace of God?
3. Does grace mean I can live a haphazard life continually?
4. How can I be more gracious towards others?
5. How will I teach others about the grace of God?

DAY 13

Are you despised?

"Let no man despise thy youth; but be thou an example of the believers, in word, in conversation, in charity, in spirit, in faith, in purity" ~ 1 Timothy 4:12

Being despised simply means to be undermined by people because they think you are a bad person or you are of no value. Many a youth tend to feel this way as they go through each day; they experience rejection and their views are not considered at times. We also learn that most young people end up giving themselves to obstinate behaviour because they feel like they are not benefitting the society in any way. We must have noted a clash between the youth and the elders in this generation because of this; the youth feel that they should rule the world while the elders feel that youth are inexperienced. Divine counsel teaches that the youth must not allow anyone to despise them. The Lord is not saying that the youth should retaliate when they are despised but instead He gives a clear directive to the youth: 'Be thou an example.' Dear youth, you ought to realise that *'what you give is what you get.'* You will indeed be despised if you are living a degrading life, people will not respect you if you do not respect yourself; if you do not show yourself to be a faithful young person, no one will trust you. You ought to set a good example in your words, in your behaviour, in your faith in God, in your love for God and others. The Bible also adds leading by example in purity. Who said that young people cannot be pure before the Lord in this generation? This refers to purity of thoughts, words and actions; basically, being Christlike. When you display the character of Jesus in your daily life, the elders will also entrust you with great duties that they believe you will fulfil diligently. Your conduct must glorify God if you desire not to be despised. Do not become the kind of a young person who lives a riotous lifestyle; be the kind that serves the Lord every single day. The Lord shall be pleased with you if you minister to His people using the energy and vigour that He has blessed you with. Remember that you have only but one opportunity to be a young person, do you desire to waste your youth and live the rest of your life with regrets? Take a decision now to give your life wholly to the Lord, allowing Him to direct your life in the way that pleases Him.

Personal Reflective Probe

1. How do I respond to people who seem to despise me?
2. Am I a good example to others?
3. What things do I need to relinquish in my life such that I may be pure before the Lord?
4. What is my takeaway from this message?

DAY 14

Fatal Conformity

In John 17 we read of the most powerful prayer made by Jesus Christ on behalf of His disciples and all those who shall believe in Him. In verses 15 and 16 we read, *"I pray not that thou shouldest take them out of the world, but that thou shouldest keep them from the evil. They are not of the world, even as I am not of the world."* Take note of the fact that we will not live in this evil world forever because God wants to abide with His children in a world without sin, thus Jesus says that those who believe in Him are not residents of this world. The world we live in is chiefly led by sinful deeds and this is contrary to what God intended. The Lord requires us to be separate, to be peculiar; to live lives that are *out of this world* because He is not of this world. He says that we should not be conformed to this world but we should be transformed. I have personally experienced how it feels like to be different, not doing what is commonly done – many have frowned at me. It is true that when you do not conform to the 'in-things', you will have very few friends. So be it – Jesus shall be your best friend and you will be transformed 'from glory to glory'. Transformation only comes when we have had an experience with Jesus, only He is capable of changing us to be like Him. We will only know what is good when we study the Word of God and allow His Holy Spirit to work within our hearts. When we abide in Him, He will abide in us and when this happens, we will know what His will is. However, when we follow the standards of this world, our minds will be beclouded thus we will fail to conform to heavenly standards and we will be led by sinful desires of this world. We should know that God detests sin, therefore when we do the things of this world, we are selling ourselves to Satan and we shall not be called the children of God. All that is not of God tends to death, all the works of the flesh do not give life, but if we live according to God's standards we shall inherit the kingdom of God. It is your choice, dear child of God, whether you want to live eternally or perish. Conform to the will of God and you will live in peace.

Personal Reflective Probe

1. Am I guilty of conforming to the things of this world?
2. How will I now seek to have my life transformed?
3. What are the dangers of conforming to the standards of this world?
4. How will I share this lesson with my loved ones?
5. What important lessons have I gathered from this message?

DAY 15

Gratitude to God: A healthy you

"In everything give thanks: for this is the will of God in Christ Jesus concerning you" ~ 1 Thessalonians 5:18

People always complain. We are always dissatisfied, and we feel that if we do not voice out our frustration, we shall suffer. It is a common practise for one to look at the negative things that happen in one's life and consider that life is not fair to him. We spend so much time studying the pain we experience every single day; we also think a lot about people who seem to dislike us or who do not have our best interest at heart. When will we look at the sunshine in our lives? When will we be grateful for the many blessings that are in our lives? It is not God's will for us to be ungrateful; He wants us to be thankful for everything. This verse teaches us that even when we face trying times we should still be grateful. It is so true that we have been blessed even beyond the negative things that we face. It is important for us to focus on the good if we desire to be filled with joy in all circumstances. God has done great things in your life, what He has done for you cannot be counted, therefore cease whining about everything and start to be grateful. Acknowledge that all that you need comes from God and in due time He shall provide according to His will and when He has provided, show gratitude. One way to show our gratitude to God is to serve Him with our lives, yielding our will to Him since we have nothing tangible to give. Our lives are to be thanksgiving sacrifices every single day for this is the will of God in Christ Jesus. Be thankful and stop murmuring, God is in control and He knows why we face various challenges in our lives. He knows, let Him do the worrying and you do the thanking. Research conducted indicates that gratitude helps to improve mental health and physical wellbeing (Kane, 2019)[7]. Now, imagine how much more your wellbeing will be nourished when you show gratitude to the Lord, your Maker.

Personal Reflective Probe

1. Have I been a grateful person to the Lord?
2. How will I work on changing my tendency to be dissatisfied?
3. Do I believe that gratitude can have a positive impact on my health holistically?
4. What important lessons have I learnt from today's message?

---

[7]   Kane, S. 2019. *How Gratitude Can Affect Your Physical and Psychological Well-Being.* [Available online: https://psychcentral.com/lib/how-gratitude-can-affect-your-physical-and-psychological-well-being/.

DAY 16

Perilous Times

"This know also, that in the last days perilous times shall come" ~ 2 Timothy 3:1

It is of certainty that perilous times are at hand, for the Word of God warned us beforehand. The word 'perilous' is an adjective derived from the root word 'peril' which is synonymous to the following words: danger, jeopardy, and hazard. A student of the Bible would know that even Jesus Christ warned His disciples of days of tribulation beforehand. We ought to know that before the Second Coming of Jesus, a time of trouble must garb this world, the Scriptures tell us of the plagues that would fall on the ungodly during those days (see Revelation 8 and 9). The Lord is interested in each individual and He does not desire for any of us to perish. However, His door of mercy will soon be shut and no one will be able to stand His wrath. From 1 Timothy 3:1-5, we learn that perilous times will not be pleasant at all, as a matter of fact, the deeds that will be done on the face of the earth will be totally abominable to God. This will be a time of great evil and you would agree with me that we are truly living in those days. What should be of concern is whether we shall be on the Lord's side when the time of trouble comes. Malachi describes the day of Jesus' coming as *'the great and dreadful day of the Lord'* (Malachi 4:5). As it is now, we may consider that God's heart aches because of the continual disobedience of humanity, as it happened in the days of Noah. We ought to be spiritually vigilant, lest the coming of the Lord takes us by astonishment. Perilous times, these days we live in, are characterized by so much carefree living. The youth is content with mediocre knowledge of God, they are comfortable with occasional study of God's word and a narrow preaching of the gospel. As a teacher, I have noted how Scripture has been fulfilled, seeing that the children of today are so disobedient. Many ask why things have changed these days. The truth is that all these things were already predicted. It is heart breaking to see that the very youth that is supposed to be running with the baton, full of energy and umph are now slaves of worldly pleasures. Many are truly 'lovers of themselves' as predicted by the great Word of God. It is indeed not sin for one to take care of themselves, but in all honesty, the contemporary definition of beauty is way beyond divine borders. The youth spend more time beautifying the outward instead of investing in character building. May we repent while mercy still lingers.

Personal Reflective Probe

1. Are we living in perilous times?
2. How can I best avoid being part of those who are disobedient to the Lord?
3. How will I make others aware of these perilous times and the signs thereof?
4. What principles have I gathered from today's message?

DAY 17

The great awakening call

Yes, Paul was literally addressing the Christians in Rome, however, his words are very prophetic, his words are not only concerned about what happened during his time, but also concerning the coming generations. When he speaks of 'our salvation', he is most definitely referring to Christ's Second Coming on earth as the King of kings. We can agree that as much as wickedness was rampant at that time, it is even viler in our days. These words are indeed relevant to us as well. His reference to 'sleep' reminds me of Matthew 25, a very prophetic parable that is chiefly based on preparation for the coming of the Bridegroom (Jesus). The text tells us that all the ten virgins slumbered and slept. Let me quickly submit to you that these virgins represent God's church. The two classes of virgins are in God's church, exposed to the same truth and appear to be worshipping the same God. Indeed, in God's church, there are believers who are filled with the Holy Spirit and are diligent students of the Bible. At the same time, there are those who 'have a form of godliness', this is not genuine godliness. Could it be, I ask, that as proclaimed Christians we are sleeping? Could it be that we live in constant compromise of God's law? Could it be that we are very comfortable with teachings that are not sponsored by Scripture? It is possible that we live recklessly as individuals who are not filled with the Holy Spirit (God in Spirit), the oil we need in our vessels in order to keep the lamp burning. It is also possible that we are no longer spending time with the Lord and His word (the lamp that should illuminate our path – Psalm 119:105). This is the great awakening call, a call that seeks to move us from our comfort zones and lead us to a place where we will more fully reflect the character of Jesus Christ. Today's text really sounds like a real wake-up call wherein a person has been peacefully asleep and they are shaken in order to rise. It is addressing those who seem to think that salvation is far-fetched; those who consider that they may doze off a little bit longer. Unfortunately, it is high time. There is time no longer!

Personal Reflective Probe

1. What new perspective have I gained from this message?
2. Am I one of those who are spiritually lax, not fully committed to the Lord?
3. How can I resuscitate my walk with the Lord?
4. How can I play my part in awakening my loved ones?
5. Do I believe that Christ is soon to come?

DAY 18

Spiritual Sleep PART 1

We need to explore the literal meaning of sleep to apply it to the spiritual. The Merriam-Webster Dictionary provides this definition: *'The natural, easily reversible periodic state of many living things that is marked by the absence of wakefulness and by the loss of consciousness of one's surroundings.'* You probably do not see a need to for me to define the term as we all are familiar with this natural tendency. However, this definition sets a foundation for what I am about to discuss in today's message. A few facts about sleep include the following: when we sleep, we often close our eyes and we get into a state of darkness. Also, in our sleep, we become unaware of our surroundings. One may move around in your bedroom while you are in deep sleep, you might not hear them. Unless you are pretending to be asleep, like most of our teenagers. Personally, in most cases I seem to be a light sleeper, I can easily hear any unusual noise. We get a sense that there are different stages of sleep. The point is, sleep takes you to a whole different environment, you may even dream of having billions of Rands in your bank account when in reality you have zilch. That is just sleep in its most practical sense. We may thus conclude that sleep is enjoyable; you get to rest and not be bothered by anyone. In this case, you know that a sleeping person is not to be disturbed, otherwise, war will break loose. The Bible does talk about 'sleep'. It does teach the concept both literally and spiritually. In my search, I discovered that the word 'sleep' occurs 72 times in the King James Version Bible. In Genesis 2:21, the concept of 'deep sleep' is introduced. Adam had to be in deep sleep for God to perform the most sophisticated surgery of all times. In Deuteronomy 31:16, and in other Biblical texts, when a person dies, they are said to be sleeping. In Psalm 132:4, we are introduced to the first thing that happens before one sleeps, that is slumber. Proverbs 6:9-10; 20:13 address the issue of laziness that is caused by the love of sleep. The reference in 1 Thessalonians 5:6-7 does not speak about literal sleep, it speaks of a much more bizarre kind of sleep. Read on to learn more!

DAY 19

Spiritual Sleep PART 2

"Awake to righteousness, and sin not; for some have not the knowledge of God: I speak this to your shame" ~ 1 Corinthians 15:34, KJV

"Therefore let us not sleep, as do others; but let us watch and be sober. For they that sleep sleep in the night; and they that be drunken are drunken in the night" ~ 1 Thessalonians 5:6, 7

It is important to study what the Scriptures say about spiritual sleep. 1 Corinthians 15:34, as quoted above, precisely tells us three things: 1) those who are spiritually asleep, sleep so in unrighteousness; 2) they live in sin and, 3) they have no knowledge of God. Unrighteousness is simply unrighteous living. When we live in sin we are deemed unrighteous and unholy. The Commandments of the Lord give a very clear standard of living for humanity. The Law is the character of God. Sin is the transgression of the law (1 John 3:4). The call here is for us to be right with God in word, thought and deed. This is a call for perfection, the bar is very high and it cannot be lowered in any way. In her book, *Steps to Christ*, Mrs. Ellen G. White writes: *'There are those who profess to serve God, while they rely upon their own efforts to obey His law, to form a right character, and secure salvation. Their hearts are not moved by any deep sense of the love of Christ, but they seek to perform the duties of the Christian life as that which God requires of them in order to gain heaven'* *(page 44).* God cannot command us to walk uprightly when He knows it is impossible, surely we can do it all through His aid. The Word of God further says that those who are spiritually asleep have no knowledge of God. Now, this is very deep! How many of us today claim to KNOW GOD? We must understand that the knowledge of God referred to here is way beyond a theoretical and theological knowledge. In daily living, if you desire to know someone, you spend time with them. This you do so that you may be well-acquainted with their interests, likes, dislikes and aspirations. This should still be applicable to our spiritual quest to know the Lord. We can conclude that when one begins to be spiritually lax, the results are: unrighteousness, sinfulness, ignorance of God's word, compromise, a diminished knowledge of God and stubbornness when the light is shone.

Personal Reflective Probe

1. What causes many to sleep spiritually?
2. Do I personally know God?
3. What things do I need to avoid for me to remain spiritually awake?
4. Am I usually stubborn when light is shone to me?
5. What important lessons have I drawn from this message?

DAY 20

Darkness: A thing of the past

Spiritual sleep is associated with darkness. It makes perfect sense that when we are spiritually asleep, we are exposed to darkness. As we know from Scripture, Jesus is the light – darkness is not of Him. All that is evil, unholy and contrary to God's commands is referred to as the 'works of darkness'. As a matter of fact, all works of the flesh are the works of darkness. It is not God's desire that we walk as those who have not been redeemed. In Galatians 5:19-21, we are introduced to a few of the works of the flesh that the Lord wants us to shun. Today, our world is considered a dark world because there are deaths, poverty, abuse, uncleanness, sickness and many more. One should know that without a shadow of doubt, Satan is the father of darkness, it was through him that our first parents experienced darkness in their lives for the very first time. Darkness is not good and it does not put a smile on God's face. The same darkness separated God from His Son when He hung on the cross for the salvation of humanity. This very darkness seeks to separate God from His intricately designed creation. Regardless of all this, the good news is that there are God's people who walk in the light, in this same dark world. God is light and those who are called by His name are to be light and walk in light. In today's text, darkness is addressed as a thing of the past, children of God are urged to put it away and walk as children of the light. This is an indication that when one receives Christ, one is transformed and becomes a new creature, thereby relinquishing all works of darkness, putting on the light and walking in the newness of life. God does not stop at this, He continues to say, *'And have no fellowship with the unfruitful works of darkness, but rather reprove them' (Ephesians 5:11).* What a twist to this whole matter! Now we are admonished to cease fellowship with such works. We are to further reprove such, and not promote them. We are to have communion with the works of darkness. We take a whole new identity. When we decide to leave our sinful works, we are essentially choosing the light. We are choosing Jesus over Satan. The battle is real, the enemy will not let go of you until you go to his side. Regardless of this, we know the end of the great controversy between good and evil – light, good, Jesus has already won.

Personal Reflective Probe

1. What works of the flesh do I need to part ways with?
2. Am I walking in the light or in darkness?
3. Do I desire to be one who reproves rather than condone the works of darkness?
4. Do I know that the devil is the ruler of darkness? Am I prepared to distance myself from him?
5. What important lessons have I drawn from this message?

DAY 21

Redeem the time!

What do you normally do when you are due to submit something a month or more from the time you receive the task? Chances are you will put it off for some other time. Believe me, I have a personal experience of the disadvantages of this habit. When you finally get in the mood of doing it, you have nothing but pressure that leads you to do a sloppy job. I do think that most of us have a problem of procrastination in various areas of our lives. This is a terrible habit of shunning some duty for a later time; this we do because we reckon that we have plenty of time in our hands. It is a sad reality. Sadly, this same scenario is true in the lives of many professed Christians today. We do think that we have a lot of time in our hands. Of all people, we should know better, for we know what the Bible says about how little a time we have. If we know that we do not have much time left, we will live in expectation for the end of time. We will seek to live righteously, expecting Jesus' soon return. We should also consider that our lives are as vapour, today we may be alive, tomorrow we may be no more. The best thing we can do, according to Scripture, is to redeem the time! Redeeming the time simply means that we need to make the most of the time we have and use the opportunities given to us. This also assures us that there is a time when those opportune doors will be shut. The end will surely come. Ephesians 5:14 is a wake-up call to those who are sleeping (spiritually dead), for it says: 'arise from the dead'. The Lord desires for us to be wide awake during these evil days if we wish to conquer evil. If there was ever a time to live godly, it is NOW! There is no better time for us to be preachers of the gospel. Now is the time for us to be the light of the world. Let us redeem the time, our Lord shall soon appear in the clouds of glory.

> *"In this time we have opportunities and advantages that it was not easy to obtain in generations past. We have increased light, and this has come through the work of those faithful sentinels who made God their dependence, and received power from Him to let light shine in clear, bright rays to the world"* (Messages to Young People, p. 33).

Personal Reflective Probe

1. Am I guilty of avoiding God-given opportunities to preach the gospel?
2. How much time have I wasted through spiritual procrastination?
3. How will I live differently going forward?
4. How will I share this message with others?
5. What great lessons have I derived from this message?

DAY 22

Commissioned

I am so tired of the misery in this world, it pains my heart to see the world as it is now. Dear friend, it is painful to witness the evilness of the world we live in. Right in front of your eyes, totally degrading actions take place daylight. Will the world be this way forever? Let us a take a moment down memory lane: At some point in history, the earth was perfect because God created it, mind you, there is no imperfection with Him. The Lord intended for humanity to live in a sinless world, where He would be their God and them His people. We also remember that He had to destroy the earth through a flood in the days of Noah because mankind was terribly sinful. However, we also know that He sent His Son on earth to die for the salvation of humanity – this was Christ's first advent. The Word of God plainly proclaims that Jesus Christ shall soon return to take His own children home and re-create this sin-struck world (see John 14:1-3 and Revelation 21:1-4). Praise the Lord that we have the Great Hope in Christ Jesus for He shall come and take away all the pain we are experiencing in this world, He shall wipe away all our tears. One may ask, 'Is Jesus coming back to take everyone with Him?' The Bible tells us only the one who believes in Him shall not perish but will have everlasting life, therefore, Jesus shall come only for those who are ready to meet Him. Those who have tasted the goodness of the Lord in their lives and have discovered the great plan of God to restore man back to His image, will in no way keep the truth to themselves. How then does Jesus Christ make sure that everyone has an equal chance to be saved? He bids us Christians, to proclaim His gospel to all nations. If we claim to know Jesus, then we have a responsibility to be witnesses of His greatness to others who may be in the dark. We will surely be held accountable for not sharing the gospel as commissioned by God. If we have unconditional love for our fellow brothers and sisters, we will be unsettled when they do not know the Lord. I pray that we may come out of our closets and blow the gospel trumpet loud.

Commissioned Again

There is a story in the book of Acts 14 that touches me tremendously. Through this story, we shall discover what it really means to *'go therefore'* for the Lord. Paul and Barnabas were committed to preaching the good news of their Saviour Jesus Christ even in un-entered areas. Take note that they began first in Antioch (chapter 13) where they were rejected. Chapter 14 begins by giving us an impression that though Paul and Barnabas were rejected in Antioch, they never gave up, they simply moved to a new location, Iconium, to proclaim the good news. Such love for the Lord? Do we have the same love for Jesus that nothing shall stop us from telling others about Him? The Lord performed great miracles through them and many believed and were saved. We are further told that the Jews perceived that many people will eventually believe in Jesus Christ whom they persecuted and crucified, they began influencing others to also reject these men of God. Let me tell you something, my dear friend, Satan will not relax while you are serving God genuinely, he will try by all means to silence you. I am truly blessed by the boldness of these apostles, we need to have the same too. We need to stand for God no matter how hard it may be, regardless of margins and limitations. When you continue to read the chapter, you discover that soon the Jews planned to stone these men – do you think this frightened them? No, instead they re-located once again to Lystra, there they even healed a man who was crippled all his life. The Bible tells us that people marvelled at this, they even began to worship these men of God but Paul rebuked them, preaching the gospel that

Jesus Christ is the one to be lifted up. Later on, we read that Paul was stoned but he did not die. One may consider that up to this point, these men had all the right to stop this work of ministry for they were rejected everywhere they went but, amazingly so, we are told that they continued to preach the gospel. They even went **back** to the cities where they were cast out initially to continue where they had left off. When you take a closer look at this story, you realise that you have not done anything for God yet. Paul and Barnabas did not care whether they lost their lives or not because they knew that even if they died, the Lord would be glorified still. They cared so much about the souls that were dying because of lack of knowledge, through the power of the Holy Spirit, lives were changed. I also believe that the Lord can use us today to proclaim His truth to this dying world. As He has given us the great commission to 'go therefore and preach the word,' He will not let us do it on our own. He will protect us when our lives are in danger for His name's sake. He has given us power therefore we can go boldly, fearing neither death nor Satan himself. Let us not be selfish with the truth that we know but rather let us have a burden for other souls who need this truth. Jesus Christ is our Saviour, the whole world must know this then the end shall come. Move away from your place of comfort and start serving the Lord, start preaching this gospel through your own lifestyle, sacrifice your time to talk to someone who seems stranded. Do you not know that you shall be accountable to God for all the souls that you left to perish because you thought they are not your responsibility? To all of us has been entrusted this gospel and we have a duty to spread it.

Personal Reflective Probe

1. What changes do I need to make with regards to evangelism?
2. Do I know that I will be accountable for the truth entrusted to me?
3. Do I desire to be a co-labourer with God?
4. What lessons can I take from Jesus' method of outreach?
5. What lessons can I take from the acts of the apostles like Paul, after Jesus ascended to heaven?

DAY 24

The heart transplant

The above scriptural text is one of the most heart-warming promises in the Word of God, for a sinner. When you take time to study Ezekiel 36, you will discover that the Lord says a lot of things there regarding His people, the Israelites. You would notice that as His chosen people, He loved them so much but He rebuked their evil ways and actually expressed His fury towards them. God is love yet at the same time, He is a God of justice and this we see in His dealings with the Israelites in the Bible (This thought is thoroughly expounded in my book, *A loving and just God: Exploring God's unconditional love).* In verse 17 and 18, He tells Ezekiel that the Israelites have displeased Him and thus He punished them for their sinful ways. Through the help of the scriptures, we know just how forbearing God is and has been with His chosen people. We see how they hurt Him to an extent that He would give them up to their enemies. In all this, God has always shown mercy and compassion towards His people – please take note of Ezekiel 36:21, *"But I had pity for mine holy name, which the house of Israel had profaned among the heathen, whither they went."* Here we have it, God does not want His name to be dragged into the mud by His own creatures, He would rather save His holy name. However, also note that He cares about mankind hence it is His aim that as He shows pity for His name, man should repent at the same time. God's plan is that the heathen nations will come to know Him and be transformed for their good. It is never His plan to let people perish but to save their lives – that's God. The Lord presents the sins of the Israelites, He tells Ezekiel what they have done and He also gives him His plan regarding the situation. He says that they should give up sin, they should cease worshipping idols and only serve Him, the one and only true God. Then He gives them a promise that if they turn away from their wicked ways, He will purify them, He will give them a new heart. Dear friend, this is amazing! God seems to be talking about an impossible thing here, a new heart, really? You must have heard about Dr. Christiaan Neethling Barnard (1922-2001) who is known to have performed the first human-to-human heart transplant in the world. Surely the world still respects him to this day because he performed one of the most dangerous operations ever – a matter of life and death. What strikes me the most is that when a heart transplant is performed, the aim is to save the life of a dying patient suffering from heart failure or such related problem. However, one human heart is replaced with another. Think about it. Chances of one living after this surgery is performed are slim. Practically speaking, it is against nature for one's heart to be removed and replaced with another. Now God says, "I will give you a new heart." Was this promise only for the actual Israelites? The answer is no, it is for us too. The Creator, whose promises never fail, knows exactly what He is talking about. God will not physically remove the heart but He will purify your desires, He will inspire you to be fully committed to Him, that is, to love Him with your all. Now when God removes your own sinful heart, whose heart does He give you? His own heart. Amen. It means that your thoughts and your desires will be heavenly inspired. Do you still remember that after David sinned against God when He fornicated, he asked God to create in Him a clean heart? (See this in Psalm 51) Why is the purification of the heart so important? Jesus Christ says, *"Where your treasure is, there will your heart be also"* (Luke 12:34). The wisest man, King Solomon says, *"Keep your heart with all diligence; for out of it are the issues of life"* (Proverbs 4:23). You see dear friend, our hearts need cleansing so that we can be fully committed to the Lord. If you see yourself struggling with a particular sin, just know that it all emanates from your heart but here is a promise: God is capable of giving you and I a new heart. Do you believe this? I believe it because I also desire for God to change my heart, as He changed the heart of Saul and made him Paul. Are we prepared to yield ourselves to Him?

Personal Reflective Probe

1. Do I consider that I need a new heart?
2. Do I believe that God can give me a new heart?
3. How will I share this life-changing message with others?
4. What important lessons have I drawn from this message?

DAY 25

To whom will you bow down?

Shadrach, Meshach and Abed-nego were brought to Babylon but they were Israelites, from the tribe of Judah. They were taken there because the king of Babylon, Nebuchadnezzar had besieged Jerusalem and the Lord had given Jehoiakim, king of Judah into his hands (See Daniel 1:1, 2). These young men worshipped God who created the universe, God who delivered Israel from the hands Pharaoh in Egypt. When you study Daniel 1, you see that they were given great positions in the king's palace. They were expected to carry out the king's instructions and adhere to the Babylonian principles. It is clear in scripture that these young men lived by principle and they did not compromise this even if they were in a foreign land, in high places and highly favoured by the king. Time came for everyone to bow down to the golden statue set up by the king, only the three young men stood up and refused to bow down. Where did they get the audacity to stand against the king? I find it very interesting that these young men did not do as many did, as a matter of fact, they were a minority. Are you as a young person audacious enough to say: "Be it known unto thee, O king, that we will not serve thy gods..."? Can you stand up to your friends or even a national system that influences you to do what is contrary to God's word? They did not bow down, they refused to dishonour their God and His commands. Dear youth, this story is totally relevant to us in this perverse generation because each day there is a battle between good and evil; right and wrong; honesty and dishonesty. Dare to be different, I dare say. The evil one is on a mission to have as many people bowing down to him as possible and he threatens us with illnesses, he promises us a great life that is free of challenges by offering counterfeit success. At the end it remains that we need to choose whether we will stand for God or Satan. Right or wrong; righteousness or unholiness.

Personal Reflective Probe

1. What things and which people do I need to denounce as my idols?
2. Am I willing to give God first place in my life?
3. Do I long to be like Meshach, Shadrach, Abed-nego and Daniel?
4. How will I avoid to bow down to anything or anyone else besides God?
5. What important lessons have I drawn from this message?

DAY 26

While you wait...

> *"Rejoicing in hope; patient in tribulation; continuing instant in prayer" ~ Romans 12:12*

There are moments when we *feel* neglected by God because we just cannot bear the hardships we face in this world. As we walk in this Christian voyage, we experience challenges that seek to put us down: we are ill-spoken of by people we thought would uphold us, we are hated by others and some are even devising evil deeds against us. It really *seems* as though things will not be better, it *appears* that there is no hope and all that we want to do is to forsake God and do as we desire. The only hope we have is in Christ Jesus, *'the hope of glory'*. We are still awaiting His return. The message today is: While you wait, *rejoice in hope*. I know that it is not easy for you to be happy when you are tried and tested but learn to seek joy from the Lord. All the misery in this world will end one day. We should rejoice knowing that when He comes, He shall do away with evil and the orchestrator of evil. Jesus, who is your joy will give you hope and you will have a positive outlook on things because of that. Furthermore, while you wait, *be patient in tribulation*. The Bible does not teach about a 'tribulation-free' Christian journey but instead it shows that if you are a follower of Christ, you must be prepared to walk as He walked. You are probably thinking that this truth may not be attractive to those who are not Christ's followers but keep this in mind: the reward of being a Christian is worth the wait. As you face various challenges, the Word of God urges you to be patient because in due time you will be delivered. Be ye patient, I encourage you dear friend. Finally, while you wait, *continue instant in prayer.* The word 'instant' here is synonymous to 'urgently', 'swiftly', 'without delay'. We are to pray all the time without hesitation. I believe that prayer is spiritual oxygen: when we cease to pray, we cease to live. Many of us do not know how much the evil one trembles when we take time to pray to our Father. This is because he knows how powerful we shall be after that; he knows that God is more powerful than he is and when we draw strength from Him we will be able to overcome evil. Jesus Christ Himself was a man of prayer when He was here on earth and He even encouraged mankind to pray: *"And He spake a parable unto them to this end, that men ought **always** to pray, and not to faint" (Luke 18:1).* We are therefore encouraged to pray every moment, instantly because we are surrounded by evil forces that are against us and without strength from the Father, we are powerless. Just for the record, God is not ignorant of any circumstances we find ourselves in but He sympathizes with our pain and uplifts us. He offers rest when we are weary. He offers a place of refuge when evil is after us. He offers shelter in a time of storm. He offers peace in distress. He offers answers when we are uncertain. He offers purification when we are unclean. He offers strength when we are weak. He offers comfort when we are heartbroken. He makes the way plain when we feel stranded. His aid is endless. The Lord cares for you[8]. Wait on Him, my dear friend.

---

8   See 1 Peter 5:7

Personal Reflective Probe

1. Do I find it hard to be patient?
2. Do I struggle with rejoicing?
3. Is it my desire to live a prayerful life?
4. How will I encourage others to be hopeful even in the midst of trials?
5. What new perspective have I gained from this message?

A form of godliness

> *"Having a form of godliness, but denying the power thereof: from such turn away"* ~ 2 Timothy 3:5

One of the signs of the end of times is the evidence of proclaimed Christians 'having a form of godliness'. This is one of the most treacherous traits of an unconverted Christian. Such a person thinks they are deceiving God by appearing to be committed to God's business, yet the opposite is true. Here we find the Word of God warning us against serving two masters. It makes no sense for one to have a form of godliness while at the same time denying its power. It is like saying: 'God, I give you my hands, but my feet and eyes belong to another.' God is not pleased with partial commitment from us, He wants the whole of our body, mind and soul (our whole being). It will not help us in any way to do our best to appear 'holier than thou' when we are at church with fellow Christians, yet on other days we outrightly deny the Lord. We may deceive other believers but the Lord who sees everything and who knows the intents of our hearts, can never be fooled. Beyond this, the Word of God is challenging us to be prepared to live according to the commands of God. If we claim to love the Lord, we must be found to be keeping His commandments, as the scripture mentions in John 14:15. The enemy rejoices when Christians are not fully committed to God, he celebrates because he knows that they are actually on his side. We need to acknowledge God and His power, as a result, we will not pretend to be genuine followers of the truth, but we will be truly godly. Let it be known that we deny the power of godliness when we compromise the truth, when we do not live according to the commandments of God. The text of the day speaks with serious restraint: 'From such turn away.' This is a serious matter; it is not to be taken lightly. The Lord truly frowns upon individuals of such a character, this behaviour is an insult to God. I pray that the Lord may help us to be genuine Christians, but also that we may be willingly true to our faith no matter the circumstances and surroundings.

Personal Reflective Probe

1. Am I guilty of denying the power of godliness?
2. Do I desire to be a genuine Christian henceforth?
3. How will I warn others of the danger of having a form of godliness and denying the power thereof?
4. What new lesson have I obtained from this message?

DAY 28

Acknowledge God

When we see every passing day regardless of tribulation, we cannot boast and say that we escape these things through our own might and wisdom. We are mere creatures, who have created nothing. We are wholly dependent on the Lord of hosts for everything. We need to come to a point where we realise that it is to God that glory and honour is due. We must swallow our pride and humble ourselves to the Almighty God, He is in control and we are nothing without Him. I am reminded of a system used to reference sources when doing an assignment and that is, in-text referencing, where you indicate the name of the person whose ideas you have used. Furthermore, you have to include a bibliography at the end to acknowledge their work. If there is such a system that exists in the world acknowledging created minds, what more about God, the Creator? I reckon that we need to have a spiritual system that enables us to constantly acknowledge God. Should we honour people and fail to honour God? A real question is: Do we really acknowledge God in everything? Acknowledging Him means that we give credit to Him for all He does in our lives. It also means that we first consult Him when we need to make decisions. We choose to decrease and let Him increase because at the end of the day, He has got the whole world in

His hands! No wonder King Solomon, in Proverbs 3:6 says, *"In all your ways acknowledge Him, and He shall direct your paths."* He knows exactly what he is referring to here because through wisdom from the Lord he was able to lead God's people in a manner that was pleasing to the Lord. Solomon also experienced how it is to depart from godliness, pursuing after the things of this world. He was eventually led astray. Keep the following principles in mind as you learn to acknowledge God in your life:

1. Remember that you are not your own designer, but you are God's product.
2. Make sure that whatever step you take is directed by Him and not by your own self-devised navigation.
3. Allow God to be God in your life.
4. Be a co-labourer with God instead of attempting to be your own boss.
5. Accept that without God you are nothing.
6. Whatever you do, do it all to the glory of God.
7. Put God first, last and best in everything.

Personal Reflective Probe

1. Do I have tendency to take credit for the many blessings in my life?
2. How will I now seek to always acknowledge God?
3. How will I share the importance of acknowledging God to others?
4. How has the Word of God transformed my life today?
5. What new perspective have I gained from today's message?

DAY 29

Jehovah liveth

"But the Lord is the true God, He is the living God, and an everlasting king..." ~ (Jeremiah 10:10a)

There are people who do not believe that God is alive simply because they cannot see Him with their naked eyes. There are theories in the world that claim that God simply created this earth and all its inhabitants, went to dwell in heaven and left these very inhabitants to independently take care of themselves. This contradicts the nature of God for we know Him to be a loving Father, who not only created us but is responsible for our daily sustenance here on earth. Moreover, we need to realise that God is real, those who have faith in Him will see His great works in their lives but those who do not believe in Him will live a miserable life. God manifests Himself to those who undoubtedly follow Him by keeping His commandments and serving Him with their whole being. Take note of the fact that when mankind fell into sin, there was a great gulf between them and their creator. Adam and Eve fell short of the glory of God in the Garden of Eden and all their descendants suffered the consequences, was that over? Not at all! God Himself already had a plan to redeem His children. As He communed with our first parents (Adam and Eve), He devised a plan to restore that lost communion privilege for mankind. It has always been His plan to dwell among His people thus we see Him throughout the Bible, lovingly seeking to bring His people back to Himself. Child of God, if you think God is 'dead', 'just take time to look around', nature itself testifies of a Master Designer who sustains all that He created. Do you not see the marvellous things that He does in your life though you cannot see Him? I am a living testimony of His greatness! Mind you, He is not only in heaven but He is with those who have faith in His existence. Take a moment and study the story of Elijah in 1 Kings 17 through to 19, there you will notice that God proved over and over again that He lives! You will observe that God always does the extraordinary so that those who do not believe in Him may tremble before Him. JEHOVAH is His name and He sustained Elijah during the time when there was drought in Israel; the Lord told him to go to the Brook Cherith to drink of its water. Just imagine being fed by ravens, mere birds (it was God who sent these ravens daily to provide Elijah with food). He provides for us even today, in ways we cannot fathom.

DAY 30

Jehovah liveth (continued...)

When Elijah's provision ceased, it seemed as though God had failed to sustain him further, but He did a very peculiar miracle: He had already commanded a widow in Zarephath to feed him. At this point I hope you are beginning to understand that our God is not just *some common* God who does the obvious, but He does the most amazing things that blow people's minds away. Allow me to submit to you that all those who fully trust God will see His hand moving in their lives. As you read through the story of Elijah, in chapter 18 God proves Himself before the prophets of Baal; we see Him setting fire to a watery sacrifice, just imagine a wet cloth being set alight, won't that cause you to tremble and even run for your life? That is our God, He is remarkable! I know that I am making reference to an Old Testament story and you are probably looking forward to hear about some contemporary story that you can relate to. Guess what, your own story and my story is contemporary; I can tell you without end the most amazing things JEHOVAH has done in my life and continues to do. I firmly believe Him when He says, *"For I am the LORD, I do not change..."* (Malachi 3:6). If you do not take God at His word, you will not see His hand provide for your needs, you will not see His healing active in your life when you are unwell, my friend you will not hear Him speak to you when you call on Him. Moreover, you will not see your prayers answered because you are blinded by your own disbelief. He lives! I have learned to trust in Him even when circumstances are trying because I know that He cares and when the time is right according to Him, He shall pull me out of the dungeon that has been set up by our adversary, the devil. I pray that we may all grow in our faith in Him. Jesus is alive, His grave is empty and because He lives, we can face tomorrow[9] with confidence. We can walk about the streets even if there is no food at home and even if we have no money in our bank accounts; though unemployment may challenge us, when we know that Jesus is alive, then we will be filled with new hope. Keep holding on to JEHOVAH, He sees your pain, He sees your tears, He knows your needs and He cares.

Personal Reflective Probe

1. Do I believe in the existence of God?
2. What evidence do I have in my life that proves that God lives?
3. What role will I play in assuring people that Jehovah lives?
4. What new lessons have I drawn from this message?

---

9   'Because He lives' (1971), a song written by Bill and Gloria Gaither.

DAY 31

Dawn

A sophisticated look at newness in Christ
"And that ye put on the new man, which after God is created in righteousness and true holiness" ~ *Ephesians 4:24*

In the early hours of this morning, witnesses attest to seeing a shocking scene, they reported that as the sun began to rise, all of a sudden, it set because the stars seemed to be taking the position of the sun. One of the witnesses mentioned that it was actually 5:30 in the morning when this happened, contrary to the normal occurrence, the sun did not rise that day. What a heartbreak. What a cold day!

Do you ever take time to think about how amazing God is? Well then, think about this: there is a striking difference between day and night; there is a clear distinction between heaven and earth; there is no ambiguity when it comes to understanding the features of mankind and those of animal-kind. One cannot dispute the fact that the sun emits heat and not snow – this, in essence, clearly tells us that there is order in the way the items of nature function and therefore, there is a greater force that governs them. Beyond this, I have never heard of a scenario whereby there was a controversy between dawn and dusk. The opening scenario is just created to encourage deep thought. Naturally, we have dawn then later dusk, that is, sunrise clearly takes place without the disturbance of anything and so does sunset. We truly serve a wonderful God because He says in His word, *"Therefore if any man is in Christ, He is a new creature: old things are passed away; behold, all things are become new" (2 Corinthians 5:17)*. God, through Paul, is assuring us here of a new beginning for those who are in Christ, this is a definite statement and we can believe in the power of God's word. I have taken time to think deeply about 'dawn' (daybreak or sunrise) and to me, it communicates the fact that when a new day begins, nothing of the previous day comes with it nor does it come with anything of the following day. Each one of us goes through testing moments and we ask ourselves if they will ever come to pass, but why are we always certain that the sun will rise and definitely set but not believe that trials will come to pass? Dear friend, God has the world in His hands, He is in control of everything, He knows our hearts, He knows our capabilities as well as our weaknesses; the same God promises to make us anew only if we are IN Him. We understand that the concept 'in Christ' means that we are contained by Him (in literal terms we would say that Christ is a container and we are the contents). This implies that our thoughts, our words and our actions will solely be influenced by Jesus Christ. Therefore the one who chooses to make Christ his or her container is promised a new beginning (dawn); the closer we get to the Saviour, the more we see our sinfulness and we will be inspired by the Holy Spirit to abide in Christ our Redeemer. Just as a new day brings a new beginning, so does being *in* Christ guarantees purification, justification, sanctification and glorification. It pleases God when we relinquish our sinful ways and follow Him whole-heartedly. However, He knows about our natural tendency to sin but He stands before us to assure us of His strength that is made perfect in our weakness. It is not in His plans that any one of us should perish, He cares so much about us more than we even care about ourselves, but one who dwells in past mistakes and worries a lot about the future, will miss the 'dawn moment' God is administering presently. It is my prayer that we may all realise how powerful God is, He has the power to give us a new beginning when we have gone astray and have a desire to come back home.

Personal Reflective Probe

1. What do the following words mean to me as a Christian?
   a) Justification (justified)
   b) Sanctification (sanctified)
   c) Glorification (glorified)
2. Am I really 'in Christ'?

DAY 32

Freedom only in Christ Jesus

The world's concept of true freedom is being liberated from oppression, discrimination and inequality. The reality is that it does not seem as though this kind of freedom shall be completely attained anytime soon. The youth has their own concept of freedom and that is, being able to do all that their hearts desire without being hindered by anyone. Indeed, everyone wants to be free, even the Constitutions of different countries express 'freedom.' Permit me to say that as Christians we ought to look forward to a much higher concept of freedom and that is, freedom from the bondage of sin. One may live in this world under terrible oppression in the flesh yet inherit the kingdom of God at the end of time because he lived according to the will of God. What I am saying is that living lives that are pleasing to God should be our greatest concern; by the way, things like oppression and discrimination are the results of sin in the world. This then tells us that the world's problem is sin and there is only one solution to this kind of problem, Christ Jesus. Jesus is the Truth, according to John 14:6. We are assured that when we know Jesus Christ personally, we shall be set free. Satan's plan is to make us captives, he wants us to live in sin and neglect our Saviour so that we may lose the kingdom of God. On the contrary, God's plan is for us to live eternally and be set free from the evil one. To further address this, John 8:36 says, *'If the Son sets you free, you shall be free indeed.'* Only those who accept Jesus as their personal Lord and Saviour will receive this definite freedom. The Bible is full of promises for those who forsake their wicked ways to follow Jesus, Romans 8:1 says to us: *"There is therefore now no condemnation to those who are in Christ Jesus, who do not walk according to the flesh, but according to the Spirit."* God is in the business of saving His people from the hands of the enemy but if we seem to love the experience, doing as we please thinking that this will last forever, He will not compel us to change our ways. The message is clear: *'Come to me all you, all you who labour and are heavy laden...'* (Matthew 11:28a). There are no evil chains that are too complex for God to break, freedom is in Him, let us run to Him. Cease self-pity and RISE.

Personal Reflective Probe

1. Do I long to be free from the bondage of the enemy?
2. Do I have faith in Jesus' power to set me free from the bondage of sin?
3. Am I willing to let go of things that have bound me?
4. How can I best lift Jesus as the Salvation of the bound?
5. What is my takeaway from today's message?

DAY 33

The divine pace

> *"Elias was a man subject to like passions as we are, and he prayed earnestly that it might not rain: and it rained not on the earth by the space of three years and six months. And he prayed again, and the heaven gave rain, and the earth brought forth her fruit."* ~ James 5:17, 18

I know that things are not always pleasant, we go through so much in life and at times we feel like there is no God. This is a genuine feeling from human perspective simply because our minds are finite and imperfect, but I am writing this note to assure you that God is always there. Yes, it appears as though He is not there, but think about this: Why is it that when all is well then you are convinced that surely there is a God watching over you? When times are bad, you are convinced that His presence is not with you; I am moved to tell you that God is always watching over us. We tend to forsake Him by doing what we want to do, neglecting His guidance in our lives. I assure you that when you pray sincerely, seeking God's face and pouring your heart to Him, He hears you. Never think that God functions according to your own time frame. He answers at the time that He considers best for you but dear friend, never think that God is too slow to respond to your petitions. Some years back, I started praying about a very important matter that concerned my family and during that period, a lot happened that was discouraging me. Regardless of all that, I committed myself to praying until something happens, there were days when tears would not cease rolling down my cheeks as I pleaded with the Lord to fix things. I kept asking the Lord to tell me when things would be fine and believe me, no angel came down from heaven, but I kept praying without ceasing. With confidence today, I am able to stand tall and say, GOD ANSWERS PRAYERS no matter how long it may take, He knows the right time. The Lord answered my prayer after a few years and I am at peace because I know that to God it was not that long – He works at His own divine pace that is without fault. He is right on time! My friend, you need to teach yourself to *'take your burden to the Lord and leave it there'*[10], do not attempt to assist God. He is more than capable to take care of your worries, let Him be God in your life. Keep praying, keep on doing His will and see what He will do for you. Remember that God knows what is best for you, He may not give you certain things because He knows that they may harm you or that it is not the right time for you to receive them. Trust the Lord with any situation you find yourself in, believe that He has the power to turn things around. Have faith in God and He will never disappoint you.

Personal Reflective Probe

1. Do I believe that God answers prayers?
2. How am I to understand the delay in some prayers being answered?
3. How can my faith in God be improved?
4. Do I consider myself to be a prayer warrior like Daniel in the Bible?
5. What new lessons have I learned about God's answer to our prayers?

---

10   'Leave it there' (1916), a song written by Charles A. Tindley.

DAY 34

The Perfect Sacrifice

Not this recitation scripture again! (You think). This is a very universal text found in the Word of God yet it appears that we still have not fully grasped its gist. You would be astounded to discover that this very scripture is a true demonstration of what true love is, the answer to one of the most fascinating questions of all times: 'What is love?' Dear friend, I desire for us to explore this beautiful piece of scripture, inspired by God, the words thereof uttered by Jesus Christ Himself. One of my spiritual mentors once taught me that there are different kinds of love in this world: *'But love, if love* and *because love'*. As you can see, these kinds of 'love' are highly conditional, one has to do something and be something or someone notable to be loved. This is certainly not God's kind of love. In fact, I bravely say this is not love. One loves the other because of beauty, but what if this beauty fades with time, will this so-called love still stand? It is really amazing how God loves us *in spite of...* His kind of love is called *agape love* and *'agape'* is a Greek word that is translated as the highest form of love. This is the love of God for man and He requires us to love Him and others the same way. This love is sacrificial, it seeketh not **its** own, it does not envy[11] – it is true love of God. It is not easy to comprehend this love because as mankind, due to the existence of sin, we are selfish beings though God created us to be selfless. We therefore understand that when the Bible tells us that *God so loved the world*, it truly means He unconditionally loved the entire human race regardless of past and present deeds. This same God not only loved but He also *gave* His one and only Son, this is sacrifice at its best! Abraham loved God so much that he was prepared to sacrifice his only son to God – this is true love. God's love is so much interested in the salvation of every person, He gave His Son so that mankind could live; for mere humans, the King stooped down to take the form of a peasant. What manner of love is this? It is honestly inexplicable yet He has demonstrated it and He continues to do so. He says, *'I have loved you with an everlasting love: therefore with loving-kindness have I drawn you' (Jeremiah 31:3b)*. The touchstone set for us is extremely high, God wants us to know Him (love) and when we know Him, we will love others with the kind of love He expresses for us, 'agape love.' God gave and He got nothing in return, just give and expect naught in return. May you continue to live with the realisation that you are greatly loved by God, show this love too, ungrudgingly.

Personal Reflective Probe

1. Do I love as the Lord loves?
2. When I love others, do I expect something in return? How do I intend to change this tendency?
3. How can I best show unconditional love to those who are least loved?
4. Do I love God completely?
5. What new perspective have I gained from this lesson?

---

11   See 1 Corinthians 13:4, 5

DAY 35

Our weakness – His strength

Have you ever gone through a time of utter weakness? Such times when you literally feel weak, unable to bear all you are carrying. Personally, I have come across greatly trying situations in time past when I felt like I could not bear it any longer. Let us then say that the older we get, the greater challenges we will have to deal with. It is said that *'the taller the tree, the stronger the wind'* hence I believe that this is all part of growth. Sadly, even in your old age, you will still go through trying times. It does seem like life is totally surrounded by trials. Our Lord and Saviour Jesus Christ came to a point where the weight of our sins were so overwhelming for Him, as a result, in the Garden of Gethsemane he uttered these words, *"O my Father, if it be possible, let this cup pass from me: nevertheless not as I will, but as thou wilt"* (Matthew 26:39). Each one of us finds himself or herself in such a situation from time to time; we plead with God to spare us from the burdens that we are carrying because it feels too much to bear. It becomes so hard that we deeply yearn for the Lord to send His angel to physically calm us down. That moment of: 'Lord, I need a hug from you.' I have literally prayed for God to simply embrace me in tough times and I usually feel much better after that. Jesus Christ came on earth to show us that the controversy between good and evil is still on but most importantly, to show us that He has already conquered evil. He was tried and tested but He never cursed God, instead He drew closer to the Father in difficult situations. My dear friend, the Lord cares and He hears us when we pray. The Word of God tells us that *'The Lord is nigh unto them that are of a broken heart; and saveth such as be of a contrite spirit'* (Psalm 34:18). I also believe that *tears are a language God understands* hence it is good for one to pour out everything to God when overwhelmed because He is a merciful Father. I am so confident that the way God moved on my behalf during hectic moments is evidence that He does not forsake His children. The Lord wants all of us to trust in Him even when there seems to be no way possible at all. Why should we doubt the power of a God who created the universe? Why would God create us then find it hard to take care of everything that bothers us? Does it even make sense for both the Creator and the creature to be weak and incapable? This same God who miraculously transformed the Red Sea into dry land so that His children can cross over can still move mightily in your life. I am still flabbergasted by the hand of God that left me dumbstruck at that time until now, I can confidently sing along with the song that says, *'Because He lives I can face tomorrow.'* Do you still remember Paul and Silas singing praises to God in captivity? The Word of God records that they praised the Lord until there was an earthquake, it shook the prison, the chains were loosened and the prison doors were opened. What a wonder! Remember that even the winds and the waves obey His voice. The Apostle Paul speaks so confidently about God and we read from 2 Corinthians 12:9, *"And He said unto me, 'My grace is sufficient for thee: for my strength is made perfect in weakness.' Most gladly therefore will I rather glory in my infirmities, that the power of Christ may rest upon me."* Who would rejoice when he has no money in the bank to sustain him for the rest of the month? Who would rejoice when there is no peace at home? Paul came to the realisation that God is powerful therefore, he learned to surrender his weaknesses to God and concentrate on being joyful. He also knows that *'the trying of his faith worketh patience*[12]*;'* the Lord is not ignorant of our burdens, He only wants us to trust Him. He wants us to acknowledge that He is capable, and we are only but human beings. Let God carry your burdens, let Him worry about what you shall eat tomorrow, how you shall settle those bills and how your loved ones' hearts shall be transformed, accepting the Lord as their Saviour. Keep the faith in Him and He will never disappoint you.

Personal Reflective Probe

1. Do I believe in God's omnipotence?
2. In times of weakness, who or what do I turn to for strength?
3. Do I usually call on God in times of trouble?
4. How can I best share this message with others?
5. What lessons have I drawn from today's message?

---

12   See James 1:3

DAY 36

Peculiar youth

It is so lovely to be a young person, don't you agree? Even the elderly often wish they could be forever young. In your youth you feel like you have all time in the world to do whatever you want to do, you have all the energy a person can have to do as his heart desires. Tell you what, when one is younger, one does not wish to grow up because the older you are, the more responsibilities you have on your shoulders. Not so long ago I was a university student under my parents' care; I did not have to stress about what we shall eat the following day or how bills will be paid up. I really miss those moments and now, as a working young lady, I am overwhelmed by deadlines and paperwork as well as bills to pay – what happened to all that free time I had a few years ago? What happened to the debt-less record I used to have? Dear friend, take note of the fact that all of us by the grace of God, go through youthful years for a purpose. There are things that you need to do in your youth that you will not be able to do when you are much older, hence you ought to use that moment fruitfully. I am really concerned about the lifestyle that many of our young people lead today. We all know how young people have used democracy as a reason for their waywardness.

Young people love freedom, they want to do as they please simply because we are living in a democratic country. Our streets are full of young people who have dropped out of school because they feel like it is just a waste of time. Some of the students I have taught have eventually dropped out of school. Is this really a way to enjoy one's youth? Well, honestly, we do not marvel at all these things that are happening around us because we know that the end is nigh, our Lord and Saviour Jesus Christ is even at the door. It only hurts to see that a majority of the youth in this world is carefree; they have disregarded the Lord and His ways. How many young people in this world fear the Lord? We need peculiar young people who will not be moved by any intimidation from the evil one, we need a youth that will stand for Jesus in this perverse generation. The Lord shall bring every work into judgment. Enjoying our youth does not mean wasting our lives in alcohol, promiscuous activities, criminal deeds and so forth. A young person who lives a life that pleases God is the happiest in this world. The Lord is calling forth young people to serve Him with their all while there is still breath in them. Are you a young person? Then I challenge you to be a different kind of a youth – strive to be peculiar, care less about what others may say about your character but care much about what the Lord says about you. Commit yourself to use your God-given gifts to empower others; seek the Lord while He may be found[13]; be a living testimony to those who have no hope. May the Lord help you to be the person He wants you to be.

Ellen G. White puts it plainly and challenging when she says, *"God wants the youth to become men of earnest mind, to be prepared for action in His noble work, and fitted to bear responsibilities. God calls for young men with hearts uncorrupted, strong and brave, and determined to fight manfully in the struggle before them, that they may glorify God, and bless humanity"* (Messages to Young People, p.21).

---

13   See Isaiah 55:6

Personal Reflective Probe

1. Am I a peculiar kind of youth?
2. What things do I need to forsake so that I may be the light to others?
3. How do I intend to influence others in the right path?
4. Am I ready and willing to be different from the rest?
5. What new lessons have I drawn from today's message?

DAY 37

Flee like a butterfly

Joseph fled from Potiphar's wife. He never entertained the temptation. You see, Joseph understood that he was accountable only to God for his actions, even in secret. Many cannot fathom how a man would flee like that in the presence of such a persistent, most probably appealing and influential woman as Potiphar's wife. He simply fled, leaving his garment behind. The very garment got him into trouble, in a court of law, that was evidence beyond any reasonable doubt. Regardless of this, he had a clear conscience because he knew that His God was the most important witness of his innocence. Today's text of consideration brings a reality before us, the youth will have to deal with the challenge of youthful lusts in their lifetime, but these, the youth should literally run away from. A general definition of the word 'lust' is *a very powerful feeling of wanting something'* (Cambridge Dictionary). You and I know very well that when young people want something, they want it and they do all it takes to get it. There are various kinds of lust: lust for power and fame; sexual lust; lust for money; gluttony. The Bible provides three categories of lust: *"For all that is in the world, the lust of the flesh, and the lust of the eyes, and the pride of life, is not of the*

Father, but is of the world" (1 John 2:16). On the one hand, the youth are to be alert to the devil's schemes, his aim is to catch us where we are most weak. On the other hand, the Lord is calling us to righteousness, faith, charity (love), peace and a pure heart. If we also make God's word our companion, we will not yield to temptation (See Jesus' experience in Matthew 4). We are given a choice to flee, otherwise, we will be overcome by those temptations. I beg to differ that we can never be able to control our desires even for things that are uncalled for. I firmly believe that we can walk uprightly like Daniel who *'purposed in his heart that he would not defile himself'*[14]. One has to be decisive and be true to that commitment. Run for your life, LIKE A BUTTERFLY. I challenge you, when the temptations start closing in, you would rather appear idiotic to many than to disobey the Lord. We can overcome!

> *"Keep yourselves away from the corrupting influences of this world. Do not go unbidden to places where the forces of the enemy are strongly entrenched"* (Messages to Young People, p.82).

---

14   See Daniel 1:8

Personal Reflective Probe

1. Do I often yield to temptation?
2. Are there places I usually go to that are not leading me to perfection?
3. Are there people I tend to mingle with who often lead me astray?
4. What thoughts do I need to shun to avoid falling into temptation?
5. How can God's word help me overcome youthful lusts?

DAY 38

Simply trust Him

A chorus I love so much has the following lyrics: *"Trust in the Lord and don't despair, He is a Friend so true. No matter what your troubles are, Jesus will see you through[15]."* I believe that as human beings we have trust issues, we struggle so much to trust our fellow brothers and sisters but worst of all, we fail to trust in the Lord our Creator. By definition, the word 'trust' means *'to have confidence or belief in the skill or safety of a person, organisation or thing'* (Cambridge Dictionary). The Lord wants us to put our trust only in Him because with Him, there is no shadow of turning – He remains the same. Only God has been proven to be always, I mean always true to His promises. A common statement says, "Love them all, but trust no one." Thus far, I have learned that as human beings we err a lot thus it is not advisable for us to lean on each other, rather it is upon the Lord we should trust and lean. When you trust in God, you believe that He will fulfil all that He has promised to fulfil in your life. You believe with your all that He is in control of your life therefore you do not fear anything or anyone. You believe that whatever trials and temptations you come across, He will see

---

15   'Trust in the Lord', a song written by Blanch Moffatt.

you through. Though the road may not be clear, you believe that He will lead you and you will arrive safely. My recent discovery is that only our God is trustworthy and I need to learn of Him and His ways. It is interesting to note that when one learns to trust in the Lord with all his or her heart and mind, he or she eventually will portray the same character (being trustworthy). The Lord is calling you and I to simply put our trust in Him. I realised that I did not fully understand what it means to trust in the Lord. Indeed, the trials will be right in your face, you will be moved to come up with your own solutions because things are just tough, and you cannot bear it any longer. Why are we always filled with doubt? Why is it that it seems impossible for God to change our lives and make us feel better when we are down? If we learn to trust Him, we will be at peace! *"Thou wilt keep him in **perfect peace**, whose mind is stayed on Thee: because he trusteth in Thee. Trust ye in the LORD forever: for in the LORD JEHOVAH is everlasting strength"* (Isaiah 26:3, 4). Our countenance will not be filled with gloom if our daily reflection is only about our Lord and Saviour Jesus Christ. Yes, our problem is that we spend so much time reflecting on what is not going well in our lives. We will be at peace once we believe without any shadow of doubt that we find strength from Jehovah. At this moment I am revived and I sing, *"Through it all, I've learnt to trust in Jesus[16]."* Why wouldn't you, my brother and my sister, trust Him with your every care? He cares for you and He will provide all your needs according to His riches in glory[17]. It is my prayer that the Lord may inspire us with His Holy Spirit to cease worrying and cast ALL our burdens to Him, moreover, I sincerely ask Him to put His heart in us so that we may be trustworthy as He is.

16　'Through it all' (1971), a song written by Andraé Crouch.
17　See Philippians 4:19

Personal Reflective Probe

1. Who or what do I trust with all my heart?
2. Do I believe that God is not like man who is not trustworthy?
3. Do I desire to give God a chance in my life by committing myself completely to Him?
4. Are there any situations I recall where trusting in God benefitted me?
5. How will I help others learn to trust in God?

DAY 39

Wait on the Lord: A hearty note to the youth

I write this hearty note to you because I consider that it will revive you at such a time as this. Do you not know that we are living in the last days of this earth's history? Do you not know that more trouble is coming upon the face of the earth? You do know. It is essential that we encourage one another, share divine insights, reassure each other that God is still on His throne and finally, show that we care one for another. When you go through the Bible, you come across several references that are about waiting on the Lord. David is one of the writers who has expressed the benefits of waiting on the Lord (See Psalm 62:5). Micah also expresses how he will wait upon the God of his salvation in Micah 7:7. Jeremiah, lamenting, ultimately acknowledges that the Lord is good unto those that wait upon Him (Lamentations 3:25). Besides these biblical accounts, I can also testify to you that I have tasted the benefits of waiting on the Lord, and I continue to wait. My beloved friend, I know that there are things you have been waiting for God to bless you with as early as yesterday. It may be a job; it may be financial aid for school; it may be marriage; it may be a breakthrough for your business venture; it may be the conversion of a loved one to the truth; you may be struggling to make ends meet – the list is endless. You are probably thinking of giving up on the Lord, right? It does seem as though He is distant. It does seem as though you are not praying enough. Yes, it seems as though God does not care at all. You enquire: "Does God even realise that I NEED this?" There are a few facts about God (taken from scripture) that I would like to bring to your attention, but you know them very well:

1. He is GOD, and we are HIS creation. We do not dictate what He must do or not.
2. There is NOTHING too hard for HIM.
3. HE is naturally LOVE. Nothing or no one can make HIM love us more or less.
4. HE knows what is best for us. He will do all to protect us from harm.
5. HE always does things ACCORDING TO HIS WILL.
6. HE can be trusted, completely!

These facts should already tell you that GOD is the Ruler of all. You are at His mercy for everything. You are to REQUEST and wait for an answer, instead of requesting and setting your own time limits for God. When the set time comes and He has not replied, it is common to conclude that He does not care. I urge you to keep on waiting on the Lord for whatever you have requested of Him. It is also essential for you to take note that contrary to popular belief, when the Lord has not given you what you have asked for, He is blessing you with that which you need at that time. He will provide you with your daily needs but do not narrow your mind and only consider that He will answer in a certain way. Let God be God, LET HIM DO HIS WILL with your life. Jesus wished for the cup of His excruciating death to pass away from Him, GOD did not answer that prayer, for it was necessary for Him to die for you and me. Accept that you are still a minor to enjoy some things. Accept that you need to obtain a certain qualification for you to get that job you are looking for. Accept that you may need to upgrade your results for you to enrol for the course you desire to do. Accept that God will do all according to His will. Accept that you will need to constantly surrender yourself to God and let Him do with your life as He sees fit. Accept, dear friend, that you only know so little that your future is not even plain before you. You need God to direct you. Seek for peace of mind from the Lord so that when things do not go as you anticipated, you may still have the confidence that God is still on His throne and He has your best interest at heart. In the end, you will just realise that God was also waiting for you to do some 'growing-up.' Are you sincerely ready for God's blessings?

DAY 40

The door of mercy will be shut!

We know God to be a merciful Father. We know that He is a loving God, without a doubt. We know that when we go astray, He is ever willing to welcome us back. Yes, it is true that God cares about each one of us. His interest in us individually is as though 'you' were the only creature on earth. All of this is unmingled truth. Surely you have wondered what had happened to this side of God when the earth was destroyed in the days of Noah. You probably wondered if He was still a loving God when Sodom and Gomorrah were annihilated. Scripture teaches us that truly so, God is gracious and He is patient with mankind. We also learn that He warns before He destroys. He is 'not willing that any should perish[18]' but, mankind is destroyed because of unrelenting disobedience. Our study of the Old Testament shows us God's dealings with the children of Israel, He was very patient with them though stiff-necked they were. However, we also note that the Lord usually gave them probationary time for repentance. This was God exercising His grace upon His

---

18   See 2 Peter 3:9

people, giving them a chance to turn from their wicked ways. As we prepare for the Second Coming of Jesus Christ, we need to realise that the door of mercy will be shut, ultimately. The theme text for today exposes the probation reality – God will not bear with evil forever. The Lord will declare the continuation of injustice, filthiness, righteousness and holiness. This means that the door will be shut for the unrepentant heart – the prayer pathway to heaven will be blocked. It will be too late! The Word of God tells us that sadly, those who were not genuine Christians will be blatantly denied – Jesus will say to them: *'I never knew you*[19].*'* The only thing that will save us is to take heed to the commands of God, walk righteously and keep our lamps trimmed and burning. Furthermore, we need to live daily having in mind that there is coming a time when probation will be closed. The question is: will you and I be within or without when the door is shut?

"Remember, dear young friends, that each day, each hour, each moment, you are weaving the web of your own destiny" (Messages to Young People, p.212).

Personal Reflective Probe

1. What important decisions have this forty-day-journey prompted me to take?
2. How important is God's probation to me?
3. How does knowing about the close of probation influence how I conduct myself henceforth?
4. Do I consider this message important to spread to others?
5. How am I preparing for the Second Coming of Jesus?

---

19   See Matthew 7:23

More Publications By Palesa Sarah Mhlongo

You may contact me on endtimepublications1@gmail.com for prayer requests, conversation regarding Bible topics, the content of this devotional and to obtain copies of my publications.

MORE RESOURCES

- To download an E-copy of Ellen G. White's *Steps to Christ,* visit:
  https://whiteestate.org/books/ebooks/sc/sc.htm
- To download an E-copy & MP3 of Ellen White's *Messages to Young People*, visit:
  https://m.egwwritings.org/en/book/76/info
- To be blessed by more of Ellen G. White's eBooks, go to *Google Play Store* and download the app 'EGW Writings.'
- Palesa Mhlongo's blog – "The Awakening":
  https://the-awakening2.webnode.com

www.ingramcontent.com/pod-product-compliance
Lightning Source LLC
Chambersburg PA
CBHW031319060726
47590CB00003B/1275